Plants

by Ellen Lawrence

Consultant:

Judy Wearing, PhD, BEd
Faculty of Education, Queen's University
Ontario, Canada

BEARPORT
PUBLISHING

New York, New York

Credits

Cover, © pkproject/Shutterstock, © Madlen/Shutterstock, © mama_mia/Shutterstock, and © antpkr/Shutterstock; 3, © CoraMax/Shutterstock, © Madlen/Shutterstock, © Grintan/Shutterstock, and © Serg64/Shutterstock; 4, © Yuriy Kulik/Shutterstock and © Alexia Khruscheva/Shutterstock; 5, © CoraMax/Shutterstock, © Ian 2010/Shutterstock, and © Zerbor/Shutterstock; 6–7, © CoraMax/Shutterstock and © Moises Fernandez Acosta/Shutterstock; 6, © Amy LV/Shutterstock; 7, © Richard Griffin/Shutterstock; 8–9, © CoraMax/Shutterstock and © Africa Studio/Shutterstock; 9, © Photosync/Shutterstock; 10–11, © CoraMax/Shutterstock, © Africa Studio/Shutterstock, and © Richard Griffin/Shutterstock; 12–13, © CoraMax/Shutterstock and © Johannes Kornelius/Shutterstock; 12, © Madlen/Shutterstock and © Popular Business/Shutterstock; 14–15, © CoraMax/Shutterstock and © Grintan/Shutterstock; 16–17, © CoraMax/Shutterstock; 16, © Brian A. Jackson/Shutterstock and © Artistic Photo/Shutterstock; 17, © Artistic Photo/Shutterstock, © MustafaNC/Shutterstock, and © Diana Taliun/Shutterstock; 18, © CoraMax/Shutterstock, © Binh Thanh Bui/Shutterstock, © Jiangdi/Shutterstock, © Nattika/Shutterstock, © Sinelev/Shutterstock, © Chatchawal Kittirojana, and © Dnikolaev/Shutterstock; 19, © CoraMax/Shutterstock, © Serg64/Shutterstock and © Max777/Shutterstock; 20–21, © CoraMax/Shutterstock and © Tamara Kulikova/Shutterstock; 20, © Madlen/Shutterstock, © Richard Griffin/Shutterstock, © Photosync/Shutterstock, and © Jose Gil/Shutterstock; 21, © Grintan/Shutterstock, © Ruby Tuesday Books, and © AlessandroZocc/Shutterstock; 22, © AzriSuratmin/Shutterstock, © MRS. Siwaporn/Shutterstock, © Cloud7Days/Shutterstock, © Fabricio UZ/Shutterstock, © Florin Stana/Shutterstock, and © EM Arts/Shutterstock; 23, © Lightspring/Shutterstock, © Richard Griffin/Shutterstock, © Vaclav Volrab/Shutterstock, and © defun/iStock.

Publisher: Kenn Goin
Senior Editor: Joyce Tavolacci
Creative Director: Spencer Brinker
Design: Emma Randall

Library of Congress Cataloging-in-Publication Data

Names: Lawrence, Ellen, 1967– author. | Lawrence, Ellen, 1967– FUNdamental experiments.
Title: Plants / by Ellen Lawrence.
Description: New York, New York : Bearport Publishing, [2016] | Series: Fun-damental experiments | Audience: Ages 7–12.
Identifiers: LCCN 2015037725 | ISBN 9781943553174 (library binding) | ISBN 1943553173 (library binding)
Subjects: LCSH: Plants—Experiments—Juvenile literature. | Botany—Experiments—Juvenile literature.
Classification: LCC QK52.6 .L39 2016 | DDC 580.78—dc23
LC record available at http://lccn.loc.gov/2015037725

For more information, write to Bearport Publishing Company, Inc., 45 West 21st Street, Suite 3B, New York, NY 10010. Printed in the United States of America.

10 9 8 7 6 5 4 3 2 1

Contents

Let's Investigate Plants

From tall trees in a forest to potted plants on a windowsill—plants are all around us. Plants make the **oxygen** we need to breathe. They also give us food, such as apples, nuts, and wheat. Inside this book are lots of fun experiments and cool facts about plants. So grab a notebook, and let's start investigating!

Check It Out!

There are about 500,000 different types of plants on Earth. Plants come in lots of shapes, sizes, and colors, but many have the same basic parts.

Flowers
Flowers produce seeds and are often brightly colored.

Seeds
Inside every seed is all the material needed to grow a new plant.

Branches
The plant parts that grow out of a tree's trunk and connect to its leaves and flowers are called branches.

Leaves
Leaves make the food and energy a plant needs to help it live and grow.

Trunk
A tree's main stem is called a trunk.

Stem
A plant's stem carries water and **nutrients** from the roots to the rest of the plant.

Roots
A plant's roots take in water and nutrients from the soil. They also hold a plant in the soil.

Observe the different plants growing in a yard or a park. Choose a plant and draw it in your notebook. Then label its parts.

Can plant roots find water?

A plant needs water to survive. To find water, its roots grow down into the soil. What happens if a plant's roots can't find enough water? Let's investigate by growing **seedlings**.

You will need:

- A small spade
- A plastic container that's about 4 inches (10 cm) deep and 6 inches (15 cm) long
- Potting soil
- Six bean seeds
- Water
- A marker
- A notebook and a pencil

 Use a spade to fill a plastic container with potting soil to about 1 inch (2.5 cm) below the container's rim.

 Place two rows of three seeds at opposite ends of the container. Cover the seeds with a thin layer of soil.

3 Place the container in a sunny spot near a window and water the soil to keep it moist.

 4 Once the seedlings are 1 inch (2.5 cm) tall, choose one seedling from each end of the container and gently pull out the others. Label the two remaining seedlings A and B.

 5 Every other day, water the soil in seedling A's half of the container, but don't give seedling B any water.

▶ **What do you think will happen to seedling B?**

Write down your **predictions** in your notebook.

 6 Keep watering seedling A every other day for four weeks.

 7 After four weeks have passed, use your fingers to gently scoop the soil away from the two plants so you can see their roots.

▶ **What do you observe about the seedlings' roots?**

▶ **What do you think happened and why?**

▶ **Do your predictions match what happened?**

(To learn more about this investigation and find the answers to the questions, see pages 20–21.)

How does water get to a plant's leaves?

Plant roots take in water and nutrients from the soil, but how does the water get to the rest of the plant? Let's investigate!

You will need:

- Water
- A glass
- A teaspoon
- Red food coloring
- A celery stem with leaves
- An adult helper with a knife
- A notebook and a pencil

 Pour 1 inch (2.5 cm) of water into a glass.

 Stir 2 teaspoons (9.9 ml) of red food coloring into the water.

3 Ask an adult to cut 1 inch (2.5 cm) from the bottom of the celery stem.

4 Stand the cut end of the celery stem in the glass filled with red water.

▶ **Where do you think the colored water is going to go?**

Write your prediction in your notebook.

5 Leave the celery stem in the red water overnight. Check on it the next morning.

In your notebook, write down everything you observed.

▶ **Does your prediction match what happened?**

▶ **How do you think a plant stem is like a straw?**

(To learn more about this investigation and find the answers to the questions, see pages 20–21.)

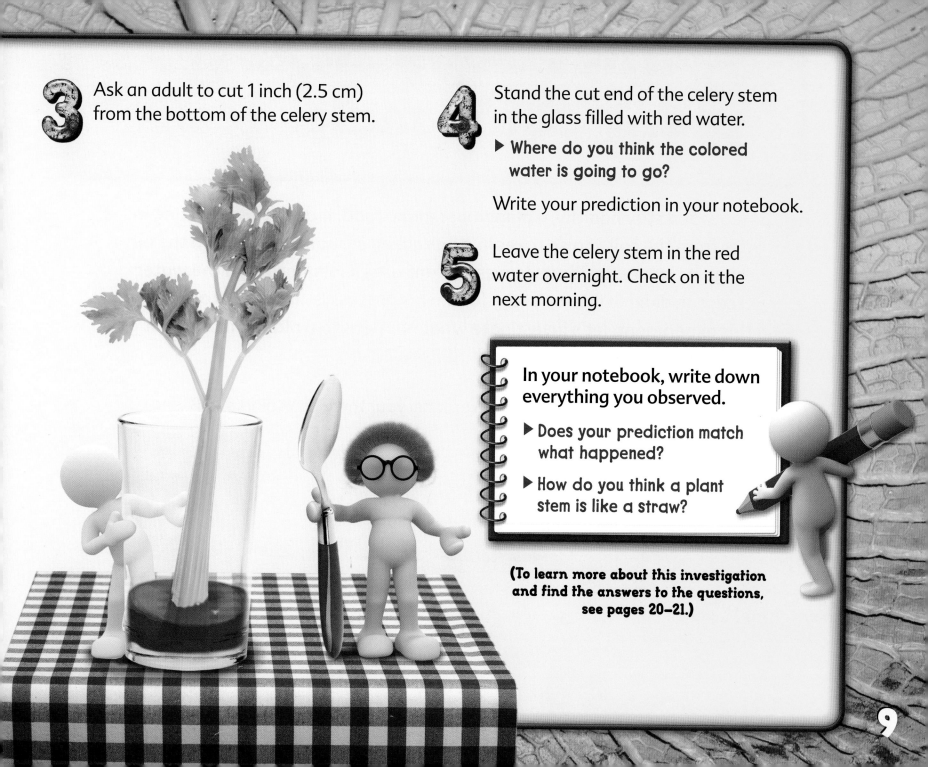

What happens if a plant can't make food?

To grow and stay healthy, a plant must make food. It does this by taking in water from the soil. It also takes in a **gas** called carbon dioxide from the air through its leaves. Inside its leaves, a plant uses sunlight to turn the water and carbon dioxide into a sugary food. This process is called **photosynthesis**. In this experiment, let's investigate what happens to a plant if it does not get everything it needs to make food.

You will need:

- A marker
- Three small bean plants planted in soil in small pots
- Water
- A notebook and a pencil

1 Using a marker, label your three bean plants A, B, and C.

Place plant A in a sunny place. Water it to keep its soil moist.

 Stand plant B in the same sunny place, but don't give it any water.

 Place plant C in a dark closet. Give plant C the same amount of water as plant A.

▶ What do you think will happen to plants A, B, and C?

In your notebook, write down your predictions for each plant.

 Every two or three days, check on your plants and compare how they are doing. Be sure to keep watering plants A and C whenever the soil feels dry. Be patient. It might take a week or more before you notice any changes.

In your notebook, write down what you observed.

▶ After one week, which plant looks the healthiest? Which plant looks the unhealthiest?

▶ What do the plants look like after two weeks?

▶ What do the appearances of plants B and C tell you about how plants use the food they make?

(To learn more about this investigation and find the answers to the questions, see pages 20–21.)

What happens to a leaf if there's no sunlight?

Inside their leaves, plants use sunlight to make a substance called **chlorophyll**. It's this substance that gives plants their green color. Chlorophyll has an important job to do. It traps the sunlight that plants need for photosynthesis. So what happens to a leaf if no sunlight can reach it? Let's investigate!

You will need:

- An indoor or outdoor plant
- A large sheet of black paper
- Tape
- A clear plastic bag and string, if using an outdoor plant
- A notebook and pencil

 Choose a plant that has large green leaves. Carefully wrap and tape the black paper around one of the leaves. Make sure the leaf is still attached to the plant and that no light can reach the leaf.

black paper

If your plant is outdoors, place a plastic bag over the paper-covered leaf to keep it dry. Gently tie the bag around the leaf with string.

▶ **How do you think the leaf will change now that sunlight cannot reach it?**

Write your prediction in your notebook.

 After one week, remove the black paper from the leaf and compare the leaf to the plant's other leaves.

In your notebook, write down everything you observed.

▶ **In what ways is the covered leaf different from the plant's other leaves?**

▶ **What do you think has caused these changes?**

(To learn more about this investigation and find the answers to the questions, see pages 20–21.)

What do plants release from their leaves?

The leaves of plants have tiny holes called **stomata** that are too small to see. During photosynthesis, plants take in carbon dioxide from the air and release oxygen through their stomata. Plants also release another gas from their leaves. Let's discover what it is.

1 Choose a house plant that has many large leaves.

Gently position the plastic bag over one leaf and use a bag tie to hold the bag in place. Make sure the leaf is completely inside the bag.

 Put the plant in a cool place overnight.

▶ **What do you think you will find inside the bag?**

Write your prediction in your notebook.

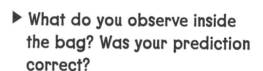 The next morning, carefully remove the bag and check inside of it.

▶ **What do you observe inside the bag? Was your prediction correct?**

▶ **What do you think has happened?**

▶ **Where did the substance come from, and why do you think the plant released it?**

(To learn more about this investigation and find the answers to the questions, see pages 20–21.)

15

What seed shapes float in the wind?

In order to **reproduce**, plants make seeds. A seed needs soil, water, nutrients, and sunlight to grow. If too many seeds try to grow in the same spot, there won't be enough **resources** for all of them to survive. So plants have developed different ways to spread their seeds. Many plants, such as dandelions, use the wind. Each dandelion seed has a tiny, fluffy parachute that helps it float to a new growing place. In this investigation, you will design a seed that can be carried by the wind.

You will need:

- A notebook and a pencil
- Craft materials such as modeling clay, string, construction paper, beads, and feathers
- Scissors
- Glue or tape
- A ruler

Think about different seed shapes.

▶ **What shape of seed do you think will float best in the wind?**

▶ **Should the seed be heavy or light?**

▶ **Will the seed have any special parts to help it stay in the air?**

Write down and also sketch your ideas in your notebook.

Use craft materials, scissors, and glue or tape to make three different seeds.

▶ **Which of your designs do you think will float best in the air?**

In your notebook, record your predictions for how well each one will float.

Carry your seeds to an open area in a room. Place one seed in the palm of your hand. Blow hard on the seed. Using a ruler, measure the distance from where you are standing to the seed's landing place.

▶ **How far did the seed travel?**

Record the distance in your notebook.

Repeat step 3 with each of the other seeds. Measure and record how far each seed travels.

▶ **Did your predictions match what happened? Why or why not?**

(To learn more about this investigation and find the answers to the questions, see pages 20–21.)

How many seeds are in some fruits?

Some plants grow seeds inside fruits. This helps plants spread their seeds to new places. How does this work? When an animal eats the fruit, the seeds pass through the animal's body. Then when the animal poops, the seeds land on the ground and grow. Some fruits have many seeds, while others just have one. Let's discover how many seeds are in some familiar fruits!

You will need:

- Choose three of the following fruits:

  A peach   A raspberry

  An apple   A pepper

  A tomato   A squash

- A cutting board
- A notebook and a pencil
- An adult helper with a knife
- A spoon

Not all fruit tastes sweet. Peppers, eggplants, and squash are actually fruits. Why? They contain seeds!

Place the first fruit on a cutting board.

▶ **How many seeds do you think are inside the fruit?**

Write your predictions in your notebook.

Ask an adult to cut open the fruit. Then using a spoon or your fingers, remove all the seeds and count them. Record the number in your notebook.

▶ **How close was your prediction to the actual number of seeds?**

Predict how many seeds will be in each of the other two fruits. Then repeat step 2.

seeds

seeds

▶ **Which of the fruits had the most seeds?**

▶ **Which one had the largest seeds, and which had the smallest seeds?**

(To learn more about this investigation and find the answers to the questions, see pages 20–21.)

Discovery Time

Investigating plants using science is fun! Now, let's check out all the things we've discovered.

Can plant roots find water?

Pages 6-7

Seedling A has received plenty of water. This seedling should look strong and healthy. Its roots should be growing down into the soil beneath the plant. Seedling B has not received enough water. This seedling may not be as big or look as healthy as Seedling A. Because Seedling B was not given enough water, some of its roots might have spread sideways toward the moist soil near seedling A.

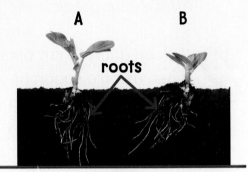

How does water get to a plant's leaves?

Pages 8-9

The celery leaves and stem may appear red in color. This is because the red water moved up the celery stem and into the leaves through tiny tubes in the stem called xylem (ZYE-luhm). When water moves up the tubes, it's like fluid being sucked up a straw. Look at the cut end of the celery stem and you will be able to see the xylem. The nutrients that plants need are dissolved in water that's in the soil and then carried to a plant's leaves and flowers.

What happens if a plant can't make food?

Pages 10-11

Plant A will look the healthiest. Plants B and C will not look as healthy and may not have grown as big. Plant A had water, carbon dioxide, and sunlight—everything it needs to make food. Plant B had carbon dioxide and sunlight but no water. It was not able to make food. Its leaves may look droopy or dry. Plant C had water and carbon dioxide but no sunlight for making food. Its leaves probably look paler than the leaves of the other two plants.

What happens to a leaf if there's no sunlight?

Pages 12–13

The leaf may have lost some of its green color and it may be turning yellow or brown. It may also look shriveled or unhealthy compared to the plant's other leaves. A lack of sunlight caused these changes. Without sunlight, the leaf was unable to make green chlorophyll, which gives plants their green color. Also, without chlorophyll, the leaf was unable to make food. As a result, it started to die.

What do plants release from their leaves?

Pages 14–15

When a leaf's stomata are open, they take in carbon dioxide. They also release oxygen and a gas called **water vapor** into the air. The leaf on your plant released water vapor into the bag. At night, the vapor cooled and turned into liquid water.

What seed shapes float in the wind?

Pages 16–17

Many seeds that are spread by the wind are small and very light. For example, tiny foxglove seeds can easily be carried for long distances by the wind. Large, heavy seeds such as maple tree seeds can also travel in the wind, but they have wings to help them stay up in the air. The longer a seed is in the air, the farther from its parent plant it will travel.

foxglove seeds

maple tree seed

wings

How many seeds are in some fruits?

Pages 18–19

The results will vary depending on the fruits chosen. Some fruits, such as tomatoes and raspberries, have lots of small seeds. Not all these seeds will survive and grow into new plants. However, because there are so many of them, some seeds will be successful. Other fruits, such as peaches, contain a single large seed that has a hard outer shell. That single seed has a better chance of survival because it's big and tough.

Plants in Your World

Now that you've discovered a lot about plants, check out the plants in the world around you!

1. The roots of some plants are good to eat. Look at these four vegetables.

▶ **Which vegetable do you think grows underground and is the root of a plant?**

2. Sometimes on a hot, sunny day, a plant in a garden might look droopy. Its leaves and flowers might hang down and look thin and papery.

▶ **The plant has plenty of light, so what do you think it needs?**

3. In fall, the leaves of some trees change color. They may turn from green to yellow, brown, orange, or red.

▶ **What do you think is causing this change?**

4. A strawberry is a fruit that holds the seeds of a strawberry plant.

▶ **Look at this picture of strawberries. Where are the seeds?**

Answers: 1. Carrot plants have long orange roots that are edible. 2. The plant needs water. Once water is poured on the soil, the water will travel from the roots and up the plant's stem to its leaves and flowers. When water reaches the plant's leaves, they will become plump and firm again. 3. As winter gets near, there's less sunlight each day. So trees and other plants stop making chlorophyll in their leaves and get ready to rest for the winter. Once a plant stops making chlorophyll, its leaves lose their green color. 4. A strawberry plant's seeds are the tiny dots called pips growing on the outside of the fruit. Each strawberry is covered in about 200 seeds.

Science Words

chlorophyll (KLOHR-uh-fil) the substance in leaves that traps sunlight so it can be used to make food for a plant; it gives the plant its green color

gas (GASS) matter that floats in air and is neither a liquid nor a solid; most gases, such as carbon dioxide, are invisible

nutrients (NOO-tree-uhnts) substances needed by plants to grow and stay healthy; most plants take in nutrients from the soil using their roots

oxygen (OK-suh-juhn) a colorless gas found in the air and water, which people and animals need to live

photosynthesis (foh-tuh-SIN-thuh-siss) the making of food by plants; plants use water, carbon dioxide, and sunlight to make food

predictions (pri-DIK-shuhnz) guesses that something will happen in a certain way; they are often based on facts a person knows or something a person has observed

reproduce (*ree*-pruh-DOOSS) to make more of a living thing

resources (REE-sorss-iz) certain things plants, animals, and other living things need to survive, such as water or food

seedlings (SEED-lings) new, young plants that have sprouted from seeds

stomata (stoh-MAH-tuh) tiny holes on a leaf used by a plant for taking in carbon dioxide and releasing oxygen and water vapor

water vapor (WAW-tur VAY-pur) water in the form of a gas

23

Index

Read More

Edwards, Nicola. *Leaves (See How Plants Grow).* New York: Rosen (2008).

Higgins, Nadia. *Experiment with What a Plant Needs to Grow.* Minneapolis, MN: Lerner (2015).

Lawrence, Ellen. *Amazing Plant Bodies: Tiny to Gigantic (Plant-ology).* New York: Bearport (2013).

Learn More Online

To learn more about plants, visit
www.bearportpublishing.com/FundamentalExperiments

About the Author

Ellen Lawrence lives in the United Kingdom. Her favorite books to write are those about nature and animals. In fact, the first book Ellen bought for herself, when she was six years old, was the story of a gorilla named Patty Cake that was born in New York's Central Park Zoo.